Portuguese

LEARN 35 WORDS TO SPEAK PORTUGUESE

Written by Peter and Helena Roberts

**For the first-time visitor to Portugal, Brazil,
or any other Portuguese-speaking country**

An English/Portuguese language book, teaching you
how to speak Portuguese using 35 selected useful words.

First edition: September 2017
v1.1 : Sept 2017

Published in the United Kingdom
by
Russet Publishing
russetpublishing.com

Distributed internationally
by
Lulu Press Inc.
Raleigh, North Carolina, USA
lulu.com

ISBN   978-1-910537-27-5

Comments and corrections welcome to
peter.roberts@russetpublishing.com

*"Learn 35 words to Speak..." is the copyright trade phrase
of Peter and Helena Roberts.*

A WORD FROM THE AUTHORS

This book was written by us after we visited Portugal. Before publishing, we have had it checked, and any initial errors corrected.

This piece of work, has been made by us for absolute beginners. We have received a good feedback from people visiting Portugal for the first time, who used our 'Learn 35 words' system.

If you spot errors, please let us know. If you want to suggest corrections and improvements, or even just make general comments, please send them to us at:

peter.roberts@russetpublishing.com

Of course, if you have enjoyed our book, and if it helped you to enjoy your holiday, please also let us know. Many thanks.

Don't forget to learn the 35 words thoroughly *before* your holiday if you possibly can. On the other hand, perhaps it will wile away the time at the airport on your way out, or under a sun umbrella on a hot beach where you can then order your glass of water or lemonade fluently.

Wherever you read it, we are sure that, when you have studied it, it will make all the difference. And remember that a language book will mean more to you and will help you to remember vocabulary if you write notes in it and add your own words and phrases!

Best wishes from Peter and Helena Roberts.

Professional Input. *The core Portuguese content of this booklet has been checked, corrected, and approved by a professional translation firm using a native-speaking Portuguese, certified translator.*

CONTENTS   5

INTRODUCTION

Learn 35 words. Speak Portuguese

Yes, really! If you learn the 35 words that this book contains, you will be able to speak more Portuguese than you ever thought possible in such a short time!

Try it and see. It will work!

Yes, it will take some time to learn 35 words, but it will be worth it the minute you arrive in Portugal or Brazil and start to speak in Portuguese! We'll show you how!

This book was prepared by us to help you get around more easily. We know that within only one week, you will be able to ask for things in restaurants and in the market. You will ask directions, buy tickets, get on a train and arrive at the required destination, and have a good time.

That's why we printed this small booklet—so that anyone who wants to have a holiday in Portugal or Brazil, and who doesn't know any Portuguese, can 'have a go'. With confidence!

Chapter 1 of the book contains the list of 35 words that you will need to know, together with a phonetic guide to their pronunciation. You will find it easy to learn them—make sure you learn them with the correct pronunciation.
Remember that **the pronunciation is very important**. Look at the phonetic part and practise each word faster and faster until it sounds like a single word. So that phonetic *desk-ool-pay may* becomes *deskoolpaymay*, which is, of course, desculpe me.

The emphasis is equally important. You will notice, that the emphasis is *often* on the next-to-the-last (penultimate) syllable of each word. On our list of 35 words there are three exceptions - *esta, favor, mineral.*

When you have learned the list and tested yourself thoroughly, you can move on to Chapters 2, 3, and 4, which will show you how to use the 35 words so that you will be understood for most of what you will need on a Portuguese holiday.

Why only 35 words?

Because then you won't have to struggle with a phrase book when you want to speak! No waiter, bus conductor, or Portuguese citizen is going to hang about while you struggle in a book to find the phrase you want, is he?

We hope that you have a wonderful visit to Portugal, Brazil, or whichever Portuguese-speaking country you are visiting, and we hope that upon your return, our little booklet encourages you to have lessons and *really* learn how to speak the language. Good Luck.

Helena and Peter.

Chapter 1
Learn the 35 words.
Here's the magic list.

Unfortunately, there is no other way to learn this list but to sit down and study it for a few days. Our suggestion is that you set aside a regular time each day with someone else—preferably your proposed travel partner—and learn and test each other until you are absolutely sure that you know all of the words and can say their pronunciation correctly without thinking. Then you are ready to move on to Chapter 2.

The List

Don't forget that, in order to help you with the pronunciation, we have given a sort of amateur way of pronouncing each word, and we have underlined the part of the word that needs speaking strongly. i.e. emphasised. Practise until you can say each word quickly, and until you have remembered all of the words.

Note that the Portuguese word may have an acute accent over a vowel. This means that this vowel is to be emphasised when it differs from the rule. It will match our phonetic underlining. For example: públicos pronounced poo-blee-cos.

1	**a**	um (m)	<u>um</u>a (f)
	pronounced:	oon	<u>oo</u>-ma

2 **and**   e
   pronounced: ay   (as in pay)

3 **are**   estão
   pronounced: es-<u>tow-n</u> (as in English town)

4 **big**   <u>gran</u>de
   pronounced: <u>gran</u>-day

5 **the bill**   a <u>con</u>ta
   pronounced: a <u>kon</u>-ta

6 **a bottle**   uma ga<u>rra</u>fa
   pronounced: oo-ma ga-<u>ra</u>-fa

7 **cold**   <u>frí</u>o
   pronounced: <u>free</u>-oh

8 **do you have...** <u>vo</u>cê tem...?
   pronounced: <u>vo</u>-say ten...?

9 **entrance**   en<u>tra</u>da
   pronounced: en-<u>tra</u>-da

10 **excuse me**   des<u>cul</u>pe me
    pronounced: *desk-<u>ool</u>-pay may*

11 **exit**   sa<u>í</u>da
    pronounced: sa-<u>ee</u>-da

12	**free of charge**	grátis
	pronounced:	gra-tees

13	**a glass**	um copo
	pronounced:	oon co-poh

14	**good evening *or night***	boa noite
	pronounced:	bow-a noy-ee-tay
		(bow as in bow and arrow)

15	**good morning *or day***	bom dia
	pronounced:	bon dee-a

16	**hot**	quente
	pronounced:	kwen-tay

17	**how much** (is it)?	Quanto (custa isso)?
	pronounced:	kwan-toe (koo-sta ee-so)

18	**is**	é or esta (it is)
	pronounced:	ay ay-sta

19	**no**	não
	pronounced:	now-n (as in English cow)

20	**one** (1)	um
	pronounced:	oon

21	**please**	por favor
	pronounced:	pour fav-or

22	**small**	pequeno
	pronounced:	pay-ken-oh

| 23 | **station** | estação (feminine) | |
| | *pronounced:* | es-ta-sown (as in English town) | |

| 24 | **thank you** | obrigado |
| | *pronounced:* | ob-ree-ga-doh |

| 25 | **that one** | aquele |
| | *pronounced:* | a-kell-ay (as in English pay) |

| 26 | **the** (singular) | o (masc.) | a (feminine) |
| | *pronounced:* | owe | a |

| 27 | **this one** | este |
| | *pronounced:* | es-tay |

| 28 | **ticket** | bilhete |
| | *pronounced:* | bee-let-ay |

| 29 | **the toilets** (public) | as casas de banho (públicas) |
| | *pronounced:* | ass ka-sas de ban-yo (poo-blee-cas) |

| 30 | **train** | comboio |
| | *pronounced:* | kom-bo-ee-owe (as in English flow) |

| 31 | **two** (2) | dois |
| | *pronounced:* | doe-ees (s as in English peace) |

| 32 | **I want** [I would like] | quero [gostaria de] |
| | *pronounced:* | kay-roe [gos-ta-ree-a day] |

| 33 | **water (bottled)** | água (mineral) |
| | *pronounced:* | ag-wa mee-nay-ral |

34 **where?**   onde?
        pronounced: on-day

35 **yes**   sim
        pronounced: seen
    Warning: Don't get this mixed up with 'sem' pronounced 'sen'
        which means *without.*

Gender

In Portuguese, nouns are either masculine or feminine. This means that there are different words in Portuguese for 'the' and different words for 'a'. In English we can just say 'the bottle' or 'a bottle', but not in Portuguese.

At this "beginner's level" you won't have time to learn all the details so we suggest that you just try to follow the rule—getting it wrong some of the time. No one will mind.

For the masculine 'the' use 'o' (as *owe*). e.g. o *comboio*
For the masculine 'a' use 'um' (as *oon*). e.g um *comboio*
o *comboio* (the train), *um comboio* (a train).
Note that this is pronounced oon kom-bo-ee-owe

For the feminine 'the' use 'a' (as *a*). e.g. *a estação*
For the feminine 'a' use 'uma' (as *oona*). e.g. *uma estação.*
a estação (the station), *uma estação* (a station).
Note that this is pronounced *ooma* es-ta-sow-n (as in English town), and sounding the 'n' quietly at the end of the word.

13

Pronunciation

The <u>most important</u> pronunciation you will find difficult is that <u>the letter **m** at the end of a word is pronounced</u> **n**.

Also, to help with your pronunciation, the letter s is pronounced as in the English word *soft*. Not as in *phase*.

The letter j in Portuguese is pronounced as a soft j as in the English word leisure or pleasure. Not a hard j as in *jam*.

The letter c before i or e is pronounced as a soft letter s as in the English words *sat.*

Finally, there is a strange Portuguese pronunciation of any word ending in ...ao. The Portuguese make a little 'n' sound at the end of the word. It is a very quietly-voiced 'n' and is hardly there, but it is. This is very strange, since there is no letter 'n' written down there— only very quietly spoken, almost unheard. The local people just slip in that quiet little 'n' at the end. So, in this book, I have put the 'n' in at the end of any ...ao word, but only in the phonetic version. Always remember to say it very softly, if at all. You could miss it out and still people would understand you. Good luck with it.

- - - - - - - - oOo - - - - - - - -

So, have you really learned the magic 35 words? Or perhaps not!

If you have not, then go back to the list and keep learning until you can recall the words with no difficulty.

As we said before, learning the list is the hardest part of this job, but it won't take long if you really work at it. The morning time is the best time to learn things—when you are fresh. It's hard work in the evening when you're tired. So, find the first morning that you can—preferably before you go on holiday—and start to learn the list of 35 words. Then re-learn them the day after, and the day after and the day after. Five half hour sessions over five days will be much better than one two-and-a-half hour session. Of course, it's even possible to learn the words while you're on holiday. At least you'll have some time to do it.

If possible, ask a friend to test you, until you are perfect.

Normally, to speak Portuguese, you will need about three years of hard effort and a private tutor. Most people don't want to put in that kind of effort or expense. For a first holiday to a foreign country, it's not necessary either. We know, because we've tried it.

On the other hand, it's frustrating on a holiday if you can't speak anything at all, and you feel stupid in a café, at a station, in the city, or when you want to buy something at a countryside stall or in a village shop. So, the following chapters show you how to put 35 words together to speak Portuguese!   It's true!

Now that you have learned the magic 35 words, it will take you next to no time to learn how to string them together to say lots of useful things. You will be speaking Portuguese in no time at all.

OK! Now we'll show you how to put the words together to speak Portuguese!

ADD YOUR OWN NOTES AND NEW WORDS HERE:

....

....

....

....

....

....

....

....

....

....

....

....

Chapter 2

I want something.
Don't we all?

Yes we all want something—mostly all of the time. We need a drink of water—especially in the summer in Portugal.

We need to ask for lots of things like drinks, food, tickets in stations, the bill in a café, and so on.

OK. Believe it or not you already know how to do this!

I want….. It's a very useful statement, but it sounds a bit brusque in English, so we can exchange it for the phrase 'I would like to have". That's better! And in Portuguese, we use the rather more polite words 'Gostaria de'. You want something and it says it politely.

Gostaria de. Yes—that's it.

What do you want? Lots of things, especially a drink of tea or coffee. You already know the word for tea—we didn't have to put it on our list. It's *chá* (pronounced *shaa*).

I would like tea please.
Gostaria de chá, por favor.

That's it. Not very sophisticated, but it says it all doesn't it? You can order some tea in a cafe already. And they will understand what you want. You'll get some tea.

There is also coffee (café), pronounced ka-feh.
Black (They say 'a coffe black' … um café preto.)
White (They say 'a coffee with milk' … um café com leité.)
Pronounced oon kaff-ay con lay-ee-tay.

Gostaria de um café preto.   (*oon kaff-eh pray-toe*)
I would like a black coffee.

And to top it off and make it sound even more polite, we add the
words for 'please' - *por favor.*

Quero um café preto descafeinado, por favor.
(pronounced *oon caf-eh pray-toe des-kaf-ay-ee-nah-doe*)
I want a black decaf coffee, please.

Gostaria de um café com leité. (oon ka-fay con lay-ee-tay)
I would like a white coffee, please.

Quero um copo de agua, por favor.
(pronounced   Kay-roh oon co-po day ag-wa, por fav-or)
I want a glass of water please.

Este é bom.   (pronounced *ess-tay ay bon*)
This is good.

Gostaria de uma garrafa de água mineral gaseificada, por favor.
(gaseificada pronounced gas-ay-ee-fee-ca-da)
I want a bottle of sparkling mineral water please.

If you don't want your water fizzy, that's easy too. You don't have to
try to think up an equivalent phrase for the English words 'still
water', you just say "água sem gás", which means 'without gas'.
(Pronounced *ag-wa sen gas*.)

In fact, there's another useful tip for every situation. If you know one adjective, but don't know it's opposite word, just add the word 'no'. For example, you want to say that your wine is warm, but you can only remember the word '*frio/fria*' meaning cold. You can complain: '*Esta água não é fria*'. This water is not cold. Or 'This is not good': '*Este não é bom*'. (*Es*-tay now-n ay *bon*.)

Quero uma limonada, por favor. (Pronounce *uma* as *ooma*.)
I want a lemonade, please.   (lee-mon-ah-da)

Gostaria de a conta por favor.
Usually shortened to Gostaria da conta por favor.
I would like the bill please - in the restaurant or bar. Perhaps you actually don't, but someone has to!

That's it—you are in control of the situation in the cafe. But don't forget 'please' - *por favor*, and 'thank you' - *obrigado*.

ADD YOUR OWN NOTES AND NEW WORDS HERE:

....

....

....

....

....

....

....

....

....

....

....

....

Chapter 3
To find something.
We often need to find places.

We all need to find something—mostly all of the time.

We need to know where to get a train, or a taxi, or where to buy a paper or a stamp. We need to find the right train. We need to find a garage. We need to ask for lots of things.

Most commonly, in our experience, we need to find the ladies or gents toilets.

No problem. You already know how to do this from your list of 35 words. You did say you'd learned them didn't you?

Onde está 'where is'   *or*   *Onde estão* 'where are'

It's pretty easy. If you need to use the toilets, we suggest that you go into a restaurant, buy food, and ask:
Onde estão as casas de banho, por favor? *Where are the bathrooms, please?* Which, politely, means where are the toilets? It's not worth learning the words for male and female because 99% of toilet doors in public places have a symbol of a man or a woman on them—standard all over the world. You'll see which door is right for you when you get there!
(Or, if you are on the street, ask for casas de banho públicas.)

Onde está a estação?
Where is the station?

Onde está um táxi?
Where is a taxi?

Onde está um banco?
Where is a bank?

Onde está o Hilton Hotel?
Where is the Hilton hotel?

Of course, we can add 'please' to make it more polite.

Onde está o Hotel Hilton, por favor?
Where is the Hilton hotel, please?

Anyone who speaks fluent Portuguese will tell you that the above sentences are basic. But they will work! That's the main thing. You have the option of standing in the town square like a goldfish with your mouth opening and closing and nothing coming out, or you can say something that is not grammatically perfect, but gets you what you want. It's an obvious choice!

ADD YOUR OWN NOTES AND NEW WORDS HERE:

....

....

....

....

....

....

....

....

....

....

....

....

....

ADD YOUR OWN NOTES AND NEW WORDS HERE:

....

....

....

....

....

....

....

....

....

....

....

....

Chapter 4
To buy something.
Don't we all want to do that?

Yes we all want to buy something during our holidays—mostly all of the time. We need to buy presents, food, tickets, papers, postcards, etcetera.

So we could try to teach you a list of a hundred different things that you might want to buy. However, to save you the trouble most of the time, you can learn two words that will stand in for nearly everything: 'this', and 'that'.

Nonetheless, if you're smart, you'll buy a small, English/Portuguese, Portuguese/English pocket dictionary from your local bookshop before you go abroad. Then you'll have a list of thousands of things that you can ask for.

Ultimately, of course, you can use your finger to point to something when you want it.

I want this! or I want that! It's easy in English—and in Portuguese

You learned the words on the list so…

Gostaria de este. (I would like this) or *Gostaria de aquele, por favor*. (I would like that one, please).

It's easy. Now you can ask for anything in the world that you can actually see at the time. I want to buy this or I want to buy that. Just point to it. What could be easier?

If you want to look up words, then that is also fine. For example, you might want to look up the word for a postcard, or a stamp, and then ask for them in the shop, because you might not be able to see a stamp to point to.

If you look up the word for stamp in a dictionary, you will find that it's called a '_selo_'. Because it ends in 'o' it is masculine and therefore is '_um selo_'. (oon say-loh.)

So you walk up to the counter in the shop/post office and say: _Gostaria de um selo, para o Reino Unido, por favor_ (ray-ee-no oon-ee-dough) It is simple but they will understand you! "I would like a stamp for the United Kingdom". And don't forget, it makes you sound so much more fluent to add '_por favor_'.

Before you buy something, you may wish to check how much it would cost. So you need the word '_Quanto_' from the list of 35 words that you learned. Just use it with '_custa_' to make '_Quanto custa?_'. It means 'how much does it cost?' Pronounced 'Kwan-toe coo-sta'.

Or to be a bit more adventurous, you could say: _Quanto custa este, por favor?_ How much is this, please?

And pointing to something away from you, or, when you have bought something, you could say, _Quanto custa aquele, por favor?_ How much is that?

Of course you don't know enough Portuguese to understand the number they say back to you, which is a kind of problem, but we found that you can often see on the electronic till how much the thing is if you are buying it, or ask them to write it down by using hand signals if you haven't yet bought it. It works a treat. Everything is in Euros if you are in Portugal, so they write it down and you understand! That's fairly easy! The unit of currency in Brazil is the 'real', pronounced '_ray-al_'.

A bit of a tip: we suggest that you carry around a very small notepad and ball point pen with you, so that you can ask people to write things down for you—such as the price of goods before you purchase them.

ADD YOUR OWN NOTES AND NEW WORDS HERE:

....

....

....

....

....

....

....

....

....

....

....

....

Chapter 5
To speak Portuguese.
Your dream.

You wanted to speak Portuguese when you bought this book.

Well now you can. With just the core 35 words we have taught you, plus a few extra ones sneaked in, you can speak an awful lot.

You won't believe it until you try, but you can get by for an entire holiday. And, if you have bought a small dictionary, you will learn another 35 words while you are away and you will be well on your way. You might even go to classes back home and improve more. Who knows?

Anyway, here are some of the things that you can now say that you never thought you would.

Quero um café descafeinado.   (*des-kaf-ay-ee-nah-doe*)
I want a decaffeinated coffee.

Gostaria de chá para dois, por favor   (*pa-ra doe-ees*)
I would like tea for two, please.

Onde está a estação, por favor?   (es-ta-sa-own)
Where is the station please?

Onde está o comboio para Lisboa?
Where is the train to Lisbon?

Quanto é este; esse cartão?　　　(*ess-ay cart-ow-n*)
How much is this? This card?

Quero a conta, por favor.
I want the bill please.

Gostaria de um café e duas chavenas de chá, por favor.
I want a coffee and two cups of tea, please. (*shaa-vay-nass day shaa*)

Desculpe-me. Onde está o Hotel Majestic, por favor?
Excuse me. Where is the Majestic hotel, please?

You get on a bus and ask the driver or passengers 'Desculpe-me.
Para Lisboa?' (*Excuse me. For Lisbon?*) Simple. They will either
nod and mutter 'Sim' or say 'Não.' and point you in the right
direction. We have done this and it really works.

Onde está um táxi, por favor?
Where is a taxi please?

Gostaria de uma cerveja, por favor.
I would like a beer, please.

Red wine (*vinho tinto*), pronounced *vee-no teen-toe*, or white wine
(*vinho branco*), pronounced *vee-no brank-oh.*)

Gostaria de um copo de vinho branco, por favor.
I would like a glass of white wine, please.

Gostaria de uma garrafa de vinho branco, por favor.
I would like a bottle of white wine, please.

Don't you think that this is great? You have learned 35 words (plus one or two more sneakily) and you are speaking Portuguese on your holiday. Well done!

And there are plenty of pages throughout this booklet where you can add your own new words. Soon you'll know a lot more than 35!

We hope you are as pleased as we were when we started to this little book for ourselves, on holiday in Portugal.

Please remember that what you have learned here is very basic and is just a start. To speak Portuguese well, you need to read proper textbooks and go to classes with a good teacher. Or even get private lessons. We hope we have given you the incentive to do so.

But if you don't study the language more deeply, you can always take our booklet with you when you go to Portugal or Brazil again!

With best wishes,
Peter and Helena Roberts.

www.ingramcontent.com/pod-product-compliance
Lightning Source LLC
LaVergne TN
LVHW051713080426
835511LV00017B/2897